The Story of a Special Day
Volume 274

September

30

The 273rd day of the year (274th in leap years).
There are 92 days remaining until the end of the year.

by Michael Dobson

Timespinner
Press

This book is also available in e-book form for Kindle, e-pub devices, and other formats from your favorite online booksellers.

For more information about the series, about us, or about your special day, please email us at editor@timespinnerpress.com.

Look for other volumes in *The Story of a Special Day,* coming often. See www.timespinnerpress.com for details and for the most recent information.

Table of Contents

September 30, 1935 — Hoover Dam is Dedicated 1

What Happened on September 30? 9

Notable September 30 People 15

Who Was Born on September 30? 17

Who Died on September 30? 27

Holidays Around the World 35

September: The Ninth Month 45

September in Other Cultures 46

September Sayings and Superstitions 46

September Symbols 47

September 30 Zodiac Signs 49

What Day of the Week is September 30? 53

On Names and Dates 54

Copyright, Credit, and Contact 59

Other Books from Timespinner Press 65

For the definition of "OS," "CE," and "BCE" used with some dates , see the section "On Names and Dates."

Cover: "Boulder Dam, 1941," by Ansel Adams. The Boulder (later Hoover) Dam was dedicated September 30, 1935 — the **Event of the Day**.

Quote of the Day

"Mankind must remember that peace is not God's gift to His creatures, it is our gift to each other."

Elie Wiesel, Holocaust survivor and Nobel laureate
born September 30, 1928

Today
in
History

September 30

Hoover Dam in 1942 (Photo: Ansel Adams)

Event of the Day
September 30, 1935 — Hoover Dam is Dedicated

On September 30, 1935, President Franklin Delano Roosevelt dedicated the Hoover Dam, one of the largest in the United States as well as a popular tourist attraction.

The dam straddles the Black Canyon of the Colorado River, which lies on the border between Nevada and Arizona. The original cost of $49 million is equivalent to $700 million in 2016 dollars. The dam is 726 feet tall, 1,244 feet long, and has a total volume of over 3.2 million cubic yards.

Generating 4.2 billion kWh of electricity per year as well as controlling the water supply for a seven-state region, it is a major factor shaping the ecology of the western US.

Background

In the development of the American Southwest, a need for a reliable source of irrigation water was critical. In the 1890s, land speculator William Beatty built a canal that crossed through northern Mexico to divert water from the Colorado River to supply California's Imperial Valley.

Not only were there disputes with Mexican landowners, the canal was also both expensive to maintain and subject to breaching.

With the growth of electricity, people also began looking for sources of hydroelectric power. The needs for water management, flood control, and electric power all came together, and in 1922 the US Bureau of Reclamation recommended building a dam on the Colorado River for this purpose.

There were numerous legal and financial obstacles. Seven states (California, Nevada, Arizona, Utah, New Mexico, Colorado, and Wyoming) had to form an interstate compact to deal with water allocation and other issues. Getting federal funding for a regional project was also tough. However, in 1928, President Calvin Coolidge signed the Boulder Canyon Project Act into law, appropriating $165 million for the construction of the entire system, which included a second dam and a new canal.

Design and Construction

Because dams can fail, and a collapse of the proposed Hoover Dam would destroy every downstream community, considerable thought was given to the type of dam and construction methodology. To avoid catastrophe, it was to be "constructed on conservative if not ultra-conservative lines."

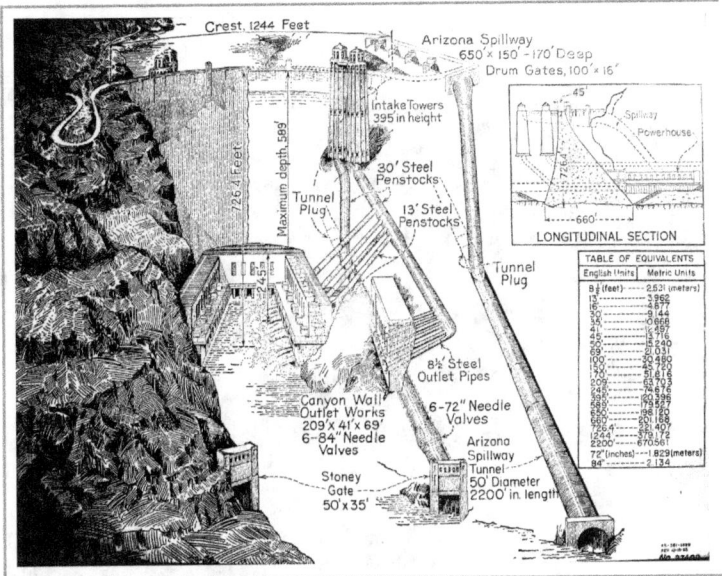

Diagram of Hoover Dam (Credit: Jarek Tuszynski)

The resultant design was known as an arch-gravity dam, 660 feet thick at the bottom and 45 feet thick at the top, enough for a highway on top of the dam. In 1931, the Bureau of Reclamation put the project out for bid. It was such a massive project that no single company felt able to take on the challenge. Eventually, a joint venture known as Six Companies won the contract, with a bid of just under $49 million, $5 million lower than the second-place bidder.

The nearby city of Las Vegas offered to close its speakeasies in order to become headquarters for dam construction, but the Interior Department decided to build its own headquarters, Boulder City, Nevada.

"High Scalers" clearing rock during the construction of Hoover Dam

Because it was the Depression, a huge number of unemployed people descended on southern Nevada. Chinese were forbidden from working on the dam. Construction of Boulder City and the beginning of dam construction overlapped, creating great hardship for workers and families who could not find housing.

Before construction of the dam could begin, the river itself had to be diverted away from the construction site, a process that took nearly two years. Workers known as "high scalers" dynamited and jackhammered loose rock on the canyon faces while suspended by long ropes. One worker became famous as the "Human Pendulum" for swinging co-workers and cases of dynamite across the canyon. The work was so dangerous that some high scalers took cloth hats, dipped them in tar, and let them solidify. When those "hard boiled hats" (later simply "hard hats") turned out to save lives, Six Companies ordered thousands of them and pushed workers to use them.

Even so, 112 people died during construction according to the official fatality list, though some suggest that an additional 42 who died from "pneumonia" actually died from carbon monoxide poisoning resulting from using gasoline vehicles in the diversion tunnels.

In 1933, eighteen months ahead of schedule, the first concrete for the new dam was poured. Because the dam was so massive, special steps had to be taken to ensure the concrete cured evenly. Pipes inside the concrete molds were filled with ice-cold water.

Overall, there is enough concrete in the Hoover Dam to pave a two-lane highway from San Francisco to New York.

Dedication and Service

Although there was still some work to be completed, the official formal dedication was scheduled for September 30, 1935, because President Roosevelt was on a tour of the western states at the time. The 2pm ceremony had to be moved to 11am when it turned out the 2pm radio slot the President had arranged was actually 2pm Eastern Time. (Afterward, he made the first-ever visit by a US President to Las Vegas.)

FDR referred to the dam as "Boulder Dam," not "Hoover Dam," because of his administration's negative opinion of the former president. It only formally became "Hoover Dam" in 1947, although for years people used "Boulder Dam" and "Hoover Dam" interchangeably.

Hoover Dam controls the water from Lake Mead, the largest reservoir in the United States by volume. Since 1983, drought and increased water demand has resulted in progressively lower levels in the lake. This has also lowered the amount of hydroelectric power produced by the dam.

Because the dam also eliminated natural flooding in the area, a number of species of fish and various plants and animals are now threatened. Increased salinity near the river's mouth has also been an issue.

At the time of its opening, Hoover Dam was the largest hydroelectric power station in the world, but today it is only 60th on the list, with China's Three Gorges Dam, completed in 2008, as the current record holder.

The dam remains a major tourist attraction, from 1937, when it was first opened for tours. By 1995, annual visitors numbered more than one million per year.

A vintage postcard, "Boulder Dam — Upstream Face and Intake Towers from Arizona Side," by Tichnor Brothers, Inc. (pre-1945)

Babe Ruth (Photo: Charles M. Conlon)

What Happened on September 30?

From great works of engineering and art to devastating wars and natural disasters, thousands of years of history have left their mark on each and every day of the year. Here are some important events that occurred on September 30. (Items with a photo or illustration are boxed.)

1791 — Mozart's last opera, *The Magic Flute,* premiers in Vienna.

1882 — Thomas **Edison's first hydroelectric plant** goes into service in Appleton, Wisconsin. It is the first hydroelectric central station to serve private and commercial customers in North America.

1888 — **Jack the Ripper** kills his third and fourth victims, Elizabeth Stride and Catherine Eddowes.

1915 — During World War I, Serbian Army Private Radoje Ljutovac shoots his cannon at an attacking enemy aircraft, becoming the first person in history to **shoot down a plane** with ground-to-air fire.

1927 — **Babe Ruth** becomes the first baseball player to hit 60 home runs in a season.

1938 — The **Munich Agreement,** allowing Nazi Germany to annex portions of Czechoslovakia, is signed in the early hours of the morning by the major powers of Europe.

1939 — The **first televised American football game** airs. The Fordham Rams beat the Waynesburg Yellow Jackets 34-7.

1941 — The **Babi Yar massacre,** the largest single massacre in the Holocaust, ends in its second day. During the crisis, Nazi *Einzatzgruppe* kill over 33,000 Jews; a later concentration camp in the area killed between 100-150,000 more.

1943 — The **US Merchant Marine Academy** opens with a dedication by President Franklin D. Roosevelt.

1941 — The **World Series is televised** for the first time. The New York Yankees win over the Brooklyn Dodgers 4-1.

1949 — The **Berlin Airlift** ends after fifteen months, during which Allied forces made over 275,000 trips to Berlin and delivered over 2.3 million tons of supplies.

1954 — The first operational **nuclear submarine,** USS *Nautilus,* is commissioned.

1972 — **Roberto Clemente** hits for the 3,000[th] time, the final hit of his career.

The first operational nuclear submarine, USS *Nautilus* (SSN 571)

Quote of the Day

"You were born with wings. Why prefer to crawl through life?"

Jalal al-Din Muhammad Rumi, Sufi philosopher
born September 30, 1207

Births and Deaths

September 30

"Rebel Without a Cause" star James Dean. Dean died in a car crash at the age of 24, on September 30, 1955.

Notable September 30 People

With the current world population at about seven billion people, on average about 19 million people also celebrate their birthdays on September 30 — and that isn't counting millions and millions who came before! No matter when you were born, you share your birthday with many special people whose accomplishments (and occasionally embarrassments) have been noted as part of history.

In this section, you'll meet fascinating people who share your birthday. They're organized by what they're famous for, and then in reverse chronological order from most recent to earliest. Those who are shown in photographs or artwork have a box around them. We don't have photos of everyone, so please forgive us if your favorite person is missing.

Some of these people you've heard of, others will be new to you, but they all make up an important part of the reason that September 30 is a truly special day!

Elie Wiesel (Photo: David Shankbone, CC BY-SA 3.0)

Who Was Born on September 30?

Business

William Wrigley, Jr., founder and namesake of chewing gum manufacturer Wm. Wrigley Jr. Company. *(1832)*

Government and Society

Elie Wiesel (אליעזר וויזל), Holocaust survivor, writer, and activist; received the 1986 Nobel Peace Prize. *(1928)*

Lester Maddox, segregationist restaurant owner and later governor of Georgia. *(1915)*

Literature and Poetry

Laura Esquivel, author of the best-seller *Como agua para chocolate (Like Water for Chocolate). (1950)*

Samuel Pickering, writer and professor whose unconventional teaching style inspired the film *Dead Poets Society. (1941)*

Shintaro Ishihara (石原 慎太郎), Japanese politician and author best known in the West as the co-author of the 1989 best-seller *The Japan That Can Say No. (1932)*

W. S. Merwin, American poet who received the Pulitzer Prize, the National Book Award; named Poet Laureate of the United States. *(1927)*

Truman Capote, author of such classics as *Breakfast at Tiffany's* and *In Cold Blood. (1924)*

Truman Capote (Photo: Roger Higgins, NYWTS)

Jalāl ad-Dīn Muhammad Rūmī (محمد جلاالدين د رومى), Sufi mystic and poet, one of the best-known and best-selling poets worldwide, known also for his spiritual and theological works. *(1207)*

Military

Lewis Nixon, US Army officer with Easy Company, portrayed in the book and miniseries *Band of Brothers. (1918)*

José María Morelos, priest and revolutionary, leader in the Mexican War of Independence, captured and executed by Spanish authorities for treason. *(1765)* *(Photo page 34, info on Morelos Day page 36.)*

Music

T-Pain, rapper and producer who has earned two Grammy Awards. *(1985)*

Robby Takac, bassist and vocalist for the Goo Goo Dolls. *(1964)*

Miki Howard, singer whose hits include "Baby, Be Mine" and "Ain't Nuthin' in the World." *(1960)*

Deborah Allen, country music singer-songwriter known for "Baby I Lied" and "I've Been Wrong Before." *(1953)*

Marc Bolan, lead singer of the glam rock group T. Rex. *(1947)*

Marilyn McCoo, lead female vocalist in The 5th Dimension. *(1943)*

Frankie Lymon, lead singer of The Teenagers, famous for the 1956 hit "Why Do Fools Fall in Love?" *(1942)*

Dewey Martin, drummer for Buffalo Springfield. *(1940)*

Johnny Mathis, third best-selling artist of the 20th century whose hits include "It's Not for Me to Say," "Misty," and "Chances Are." *(1935)*

Cissy Houston, soul and gospel singer who won two Grammy Awards; mother of singer Whitney Houston and aunt of Dionne Warwick. *(1933)*

Donald Swann, composer and entertainer best known for the musical comedy act Flanders and Swann. *(1923)*

Buddy Rich, legendary jazz drummer and bandleader during the Big Band Era. *(1917)*

Performing Arts

Lacey Chabert, known as Claudia on the TV series *Party of Five. (1982)*

Marion Cotillard, actress who won an Academy Award for *La Vie en Rose,* also known for *Two Days, One Night; Inception;* and many other films. *(1975)*

Buddy Rich (Photo: William P. Gottlieb)

Jenna Elfman, actress best known for the sitcom *Dharma & Greg. (1971)*

Tony Hale, actor known for the TV series *Arrested Development* and *Veep*. (1970)

Monica Bellucci, Italian model and actress who appeared in two *Matrix* films, *The Passion of the Christ,* and the James Bond film *Spectre. (1964)*

Eric Stoltz, actor best known for his role in *Mask,* also appeared in such films as *Some Kind of Wonderful, Pulp Fiction,* and *Killing Zoe. (1961)*

Crystal Bernard, actress known for her role on the TV series *Wings. (1961)*

Fran Drescher, comic actress best known for her role in the 1990s television series *The Nanny. (1957)*

Victoria Tennant, actress best known for her role in the TV miniseries *The Winds of War. (1950)*

Ian Oglivy, known for the television series *Return of the Saint* and other roles. *(1943)*

Angie Dickinson, actress known for such films as *Rio Bravo* (1959) and *Ocean's 11* (1960), as well as the television series *Police Woman. (1931)*

Deborah Kerr, actress whose best known films include *The King and I* and *From Here to Eternity. (1921)*

Science

Barry Marshall, shared the 2005 Nobel Prize in Physiology or Medicine for demonstrating that the *H. pylori* bacterium was the cause of most peptic ulcers. *(1951)*

Johann Deisenhofer, shared the 1988 Nobel Prize in Chemistry for determining the first crystal structure of an integral membrane protein. *(1943)*

Deborah Kerr, with Robert Mitchum in *Heaven Knows, Mr. Allison*

Jean-Marie Lehn, shared the 1987 Nobel Prize in Chemistry for advancements in supramolecular chemistry. *(1939)*

Sir Nevill Francis Mott, won the 1977 Nobel Prize in Physics for his work on the electronic structure of magnetic and disordered systems. *(1905)*

Hans Geiger, co-inventor of the Geiger counter; discoverer of the atomic nucleus. *(1882)*

Jean Baptiste Perrin, won the 1926 Nobel Prize in Physics for his work in Brownian motion. *(1870)*

Sports

Aliya Mustafina (Алия Мустафина), Russian gymnast who was the most decorated non-swimming athlete at the 2012 Olympics, with four medals. *(1994)*

Lauren Holiday, soccer midfielder and member of the gold medal-winning US women's national soccer team at the 2008 and 2012 Olympic Games. *(1987)*

Dominique Moceanu, member of the gold-medal-winning women's gymnastics team at the 1966 Summer Olympics. *(1981)*

Martina Hingis, youngest-ever World No. 1 tennis player, with 40 singles titles and 36 doubles titles in her career. *(1980)*

José Lima, pitcher who spent 13 seasons in the major leagues, known for his flamboyance and emotional displays. *(1972)*

Johnny Podres, pitcher best known as MVP of the 1955 World Series for pitching a shutout against the Yankiess that gave the Dodgers their only World Series title in Brooklyn. *(1932)*

Robin Roberts, baseball pitcher primarily for the Philadelphia Phillies, inducted into the Baseball Hall of Fame. *(1926)*

Martina Hingis (Photo: M. Clayton Farrington)

Les Paul and Mary Ford (right)

Who Died on September 30?

Culture and Society

Barry Commoner, biologist, ecologist, and politician; candidate for US President on the Citizens Party ticket in 1980. *(2012)*

Anwar al-Awlaki (أنور العولقي), American-Yemeni imam and lecturer, accused by the US government of being a senior al-Qaeda recruiter and planner, first US citizen to be targeted and killed by a targeted drone strike. *(2011)*

Robert Kardashian, attorney best known for his defence of O. J. Simpson, father of the four daughters on the reality series *Keeping Up with the Kardashians. (2003)*

Music

Mary Ford, vocalist and guitarist best known for her collaboration with husband Les Paul; hits include "How High the Moon" and "Vaya con Dios." *(1977)*

Performing Arts

Turhan Bey, Hollywood actor in the 1940s known as the "Turkish Delight;" became a television actor in the 1990s with the series *Babylon 5. (2012)*

Stephen J. Cannell, television producer and writer who created such hits as *The Rockford Files, The A-Team,* and *21 Jump Street. (2010)*

Simone Signoret, first French actress to win an Academy Award, known for *The Crucible, Room at the Top,* and *Ship of Fools. (1985)*

Edgar Bergen, comedian and ventriloquist, known for his characters Charlie McCarthy and Mortimer Snerd; father of actress Candice Bergen. *(1978)*

James Dean, actor known for *Rebel Without a Cause, East of Eden,* and *Giant.* Died in a car crash at age 24. *(1955) (Photo page 14.)*

Religion

Saint Thérèse of Lisieux, Carmelite nun known as "The Little Flower of Jesus," called "the greatest saint of modern times" by Pope Pius X. *(1897)*

Mortimer Snerd and **Edgar Bergen**

George Whitefield, founder of Methodism and early leader in the evangelical movement; spoke more than 18,000 times to over 10 million people; known for preaching a series of revivals in America that became known as the "Great Awakening." *(1770)*

Saint Jerome, priest and theologian best known for the Vulgate, a translation of the Bible into Latin. *(420)*

Saint Jerome, by El Grego

Science

Martin Lewis Perl, won the 1995 Nobel Prize in Physics for his discovery of the tau lepton. *(2014)*

Ralph M. Steinman, shared the 2011 Nobel Prize in Physiology or Medicine for work on dendritic cells, which he also named. *(2011)*

Charles Richter, seismologist and physicist most famous for creating the Richter scale, used to measure earthquake intensity. *(1977)*

Sports

Barbara Ann Scott, Canadian figure skater who won a gold medal at the 1948 Olympics. *(1897)*

Writing

Robert Lewis Taylor, won the Pulitzer Prize for his novel 1958 *The Travels of Jaimie McPheeters.*

Patrick White, Australian author who received the 1973 Nobel Prize in Literature; his book The Eye of the Storm became a film of the same name. *(1990)*

Alfred Bester, Hugo Award-winning science fiction author of such books as *The Demolished Man* and *The Stars My Destination. (1987)*

Quote of the Day

"We always do what's natural, only sometimes we shouldn't do it."

Alfred Bester, science fiction writer
died September 30, 1987

Holidays
Around
the World

September 30

José María Morelos, leader in the Mexican War of Independence, born September 30, 1765 — His birthday is observed as **Morelos Day** in Mexico. (Painting by Vicente Guijosa Aguirre)

Holidays Around the World

If you're looking for a reason to take your special day off, you should know that every single day is a holiday somewhere in the world! Here's what you can celebrate on September 30!

General Events

Boipuso (Botswana)
Independence Day in the African nation of Botswana celebrates its declaration of independence from the United Kingdom on September 30, 1966.

Dia da Reforma Agrária (São Tomé and Príncipe)
Agricultural Reform Day in the island nation of São Tomé and Príncipe is observed on September 30.

Dzień Chłopaka (Poland)
On Boy's Day in Poland, girls give presents to boys.

International Translation Day (worldwide)
The International Federation of Translators celebrates Translation Day each year on September 30, in honor of Saint Jerome*, patron saint of translators.

---

* See page 30, "Who Died on September 30?"

Natalicio de José Ma. Morelos y Pavón (Mexico)

The birthday of José Morelos[†] is a civic holiday in Mexico. *(Photo previous page.)*

Recovery Day (Canada)

Celebrating the ability of those with various addictions to achieve long-term sobriety and live productive, healthy lives.

Food Holidays

Around the world, days, weeks, and months are dedicated to certain foods. In the United States, there's an official food day for every day of the year!. Given the wide range of foods, often multiple foods share the same occasion. Food days are sponsored by manufacturers, retailers, farmers, fans, and occasionally by proclamation, and are subject to change.

September 30 is **National Hot Mulled Cider Day.** Apple cider comes in both alcoholic and regular varieties. "Mulling" cider means to heat it until just below boiling, while adding such spices as cinnamon, orange peel, nutmeg, or cloves. It's particularly welcome on cold autumn and winter days.

[†] See page 19, "Who Was Born on September 30?"

Food Months

The entire month of September is used to celebrate numerous foods. Here's a list of what to eat in the month of September!

- Bourbon Heritage Month

A glass and bottle of bourbon, for **Bourbon Heritage Month**
(Photo: Dirk Ingo Franke)

- California Wine Month
- National Chicken Month
- National Honey Month
- National Mushroom Month
- National Papaya Month
- National Potato Month

- National Rice Month
- National Whole Grains Month
- National Wild Rice Month

Religious Observances

Saint Days (Christianity)
Each day in the year is considered a feast day for one or more saints. They are somewhat different in western Christianity (Catholicism and many forms of Protantism) and in eastern (Orthodox) Christianity.

In *Western Christianity*, it is the feast day of Saints Gregory the Illuminator, Honorius of Canterbury, and Jerome.

In *Eastern Orthodox Christianity*, it is also the commemoration of Saints Antoninus, Leopardus, Midan, Enghenedl, Laurus, Michael of Tver, and Meletius I Pegas of Alexandria. (These are observed on September 17 by "Old Calendarists.‡")

Yom Kippur (יוֹם כִּיפּוּר) (Jews, Samaritans, some Christian groups)
The holiest day of the year in Judaism, the Day of Atonement is observed with fasting and prayer. *(10th day of Tishrei, falls between September 14 and October 14 in the Gregorian calendar depending on the year.)*

---

‡ "Old Calendrists" use the Julian calendar rather than the modern Gregorian calendar. See "What Day of the Week is September 30?"

Jews Praying in the Synagogue on Yom Kippur, by Maurycy
Gottlieb, 1878 (Courtesy Tel Aviv Museum of Art)

Honorary Months

Presidents, Congresses, and nations around the world issue proclamations recognizing particular months to honor certain causes. These events generally fall in Septemer, though honorary months do come and go. Holidays established by states and nonprofit organizations are listed if verified. If not otherwise specified, all are US. TTwo places to get up to date information are the current edition of Chase's Calendar of Events *or the website* Brownielocks.

- Baby Safety Month
- Be Kind to Editors and Writers Month
- Children's Good Manners Month
- College Savings Month
- Happy Cat Month
- International Square Dancing Month
- National Recovery Month
- National Service Dog Month
- Responsible Dog Ownership Month

Moveable and Multi-Day Events

Some events take place over a specific week or time period. Start and finish dates may vary from year to year. Some events occur on different days each year (such as "fourth Saturday of a month"). These events sometimes take place on September 30.

Last Week in September
- Banned Books Week (US)

- Celebrate Freedom Week (Arkansas, Florida — last full week)
- National Forest Week (Canada)

Wednesday of the Last Full Week in September
- National Tree Day (Canada)

Fourth Monday in September
- American Indian Day (Tennessee)
- September Declaration (Flanders, Belgium)

Fourth Friday in September
- Native American Day (California)

Last Friday in September
- Manit Day (Marshall Islands)

Last Saturday in September
- Family Health and Fitness Day
- National Public Lands Day
- Nickelodeon's Worldwide Day of Play

Last Sunday in September
- Gold Star Mother's Day

Just For Fun

Anybody can start a holiday, and many people do! These celebrations are unofficial and may come and go, but you're welcome to join in!

- Ask a Stupid Question Day (India, UK, US — last weekday in September)
- Blasphemy Day (Center for Inquiry)
- National Ghost Hunting Day

Quote of the Day

"The peak of [my Presidential] campaign happened in Albuquerque, where a local reporter said to me, 'Dr. Commoner, are you a serious candidate or are you just running on the issues?"

Barry Commoner, biologist and politician
died September 30, 2012

About
the
Month
of

September

THEM
ACC
MAGNA

September, from the *Brevarium Grimani* by Simon Bening (c.1510)

September: The Ninth Month

The morrow was a bright September morn;
The earth was beautiful as if new-born;
There was that nameless splendor everywhere,
That wild exhilaration in the air,
Which makes the passers in the city street
Congratulate each other as they meet.

> Henry Wadsworth Longfellow, "Tales of a Wayside Inn"

In Latin, *septem* means "seven," so it may seem strange that September is actually the *ninth* month of the year. The original Roman calendar, on which ours is based, started in March, making September indeed the seventh month. No one is completely sure when the start of the year was moved to January, but the traditional name of September stuck.

Romans also associated September with the god Vulcan, and thus expected the month to have fires, volcanic eruptions, and earthquakes.

In the northern hemisphere, September marks the beginning of meteorological autumn. In the southern hemisphere, September is the seasonal equivalent of March, the beginning of spring.

September and December always begin on the same day of the week. However, no other month in the same year will end on the same day of the week as September.

For countries that switched from the Julian to the Gregorian calendars in 1752, the date jumped from September 2 to September 14, meaning that there is no September 11 in that year.

September in Other Cultures

In Old English, the month of September was known as
Hāligmōnaþ. Anglo-Saxons called it *Gerst monath*
(Barley month) celebrating the barley harvest that
would shortly be turned into beer. In Finland, it is
syyskuu, in Poland *wrzesień*, and in Greece
$\Sigma\epsilon\pi\tau\acute{\epsilon}\mu\beta\rho\iota o\varsigma$. The Russians call the month сентябрь.
While both the Hebrew and Arabic cultures have their
own calendar system, the Hebrew word for
"September" is ספטמבר and in Arabic it's سبتمب. The
Azerbaijani call the month *Sentyabr*. In Hindi, the
month of "sitambar" is written सितंबर. In both China
and Japan, it's known as 九月, 구월 in Korea, and 腦尬
in Vietnam.

September Sayings and Superstitions

Here are some wedding sayings and superstitions
associated with the month of September.

- "Marry in September's shrine, your living with
  be rich and fine."
- "A September bride will be discreet, affable, and
  much liked."
- "Married in September's golden glow / Smooth
  and serene your life will go."

As for which day of the week, that's easy.

Monday for health, Tuesday for wealth,
Wednesday best of all, Thursday for losses,
Friday for crosses, Saturday for no luck at all.

September Symbols

Birthstone: Sapphire, representing clear thinking.

Star sapphire

Birth Flowers: Forget-me-not, morning glory, and aster.

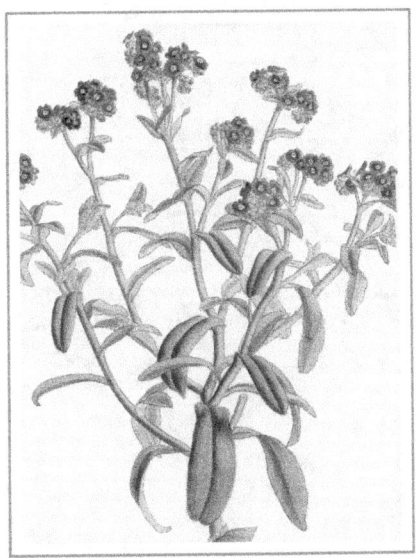

Forget-me-not (*moyosotis azorica*)

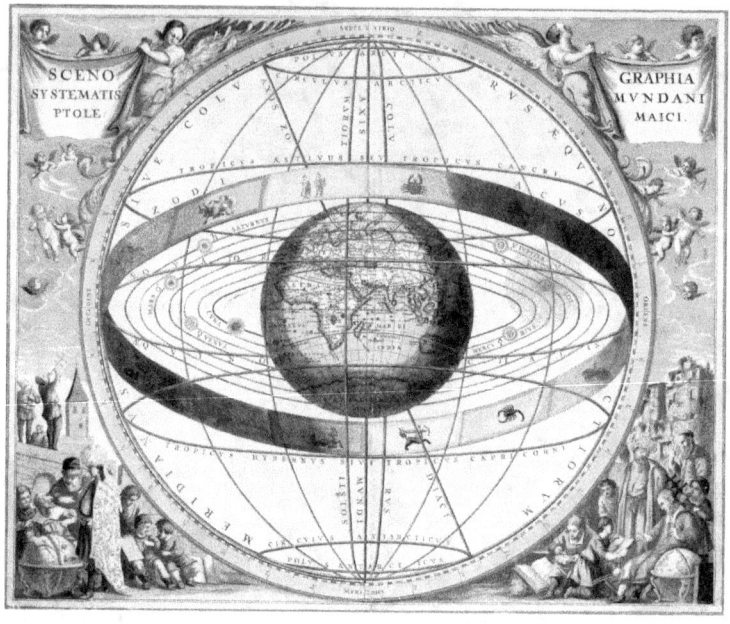

Scenography of the Ptolemaic Cosmography, by Johannes van
Loon, based on Andreas Cellarius's *Harmonia Macrocosmica,* 1660

September 30 Zodiac Signs

From the perspective of someone on Earth, the Sun appears to move through the sky throughout the year, along a path astronomers call the *ecliptic plane*. The ecliptic plane is divided into twelve constellations, known as the zodiac, based on traditionally observed patterns of stars. On your birthday, you can't see your constellation, because it's in the daytime sky.

The zodiac was first developed by Babylonian astronomers about 2,500 years ago. Because they were unaware that the Earth wobbles like a spinning top (known as *precession*), they didn't make allowance for the fact that the Sun's path through the zodiac changes over time.

That means there are now two sets of dates for your birth sign. The *tropical dates* are the original Babylonian dates; the *sidereal dates* tell you where the Sun actually appears as it moves along its annual path.

For September 30, the tropical sign is **Libra** and the sidereal sign is **Virgo**.

Libra

Tropical September 23 to October 23
Sidereal October 16 to November 15

The Babylonians considered Libra, the Scales, to be sacred to the sun god Shamash, patron of truth and justice. The Romans reassigned the scales to Astraea, the celestial virgin, better known as Virgo. It is the only constellation in the sky represented by an inanimate object — all the others are animals or mythological characters

Libra is an air sign, and people born under this sign are supposed to be extroverts, socially graceful, and just. Librans are supposed to be compatible with the other air signs of Gemini and Aquarius.

Virgo

Tropical August 23 to September 22
Sidereal September 16 to October 15

The constellation Virgo is the second-largest constellation in the night sky. Its brightest star, Spica, makes it easy to locate. If you can find the Big Dipper (Ursa Major), follow the curve in the Dipper's handle. The second bright star you see is Spica.

In Greek and Roman mythology, Virgo is associated with Demeter (Ceres), the goddess of wheat, and also with Erigone and Astraea. In astrology, Virgo is known as a "mutable sign." It's associated with being reflective and receptive to the ideas of others, sensitive to criticism, and oriented toward detail and precision.

Virgos are supposed to be compatible with Capricorn, Taurus, Cancer, and Scorpio, and to a lesser extent with Virgo and Pisces.

Illustration by Edward Penfield

What Day of the Week is September 30?

On what day of the week does September 30 fall?

Surprisingly, this isn't an easy question. Because the calendar year is 365 days long (366 in leap years), it doesn't divide evenly by the seven days of the week.

Also, the Earth goes around the Sun in about 365-1/4 days, so a calendar tends to drift over time. That's why the same date falls on different weekdays in different years.

This is made even more complicated by a change in calendars that took place in 1582. Our modern calendar has its roots in ancient Rome, in a calendar reform conducted by Julius Caesar. Caesar commissioned mathematicians to attack the problem, and they came up with the idea of leap years, and thus standardized the calendar for centuries to come. This was called the Julian calendar.

Over time, however, the small errors in Caesar's calculation compounded. That's why Pope Gregory XIII commissioned the Gregorian calendar, used in most of the world today. Some countries converted in 1582, when the calendar was first developed; some converted later; other still haven't changed.

Gregorian and Julian aren't the only types of calendars. The Hebrew year, the Islamic year, and many other calendars are used in different parts of the world and among different people.

You can convert Gregorian dates to other calendars, including the Hebrew calendar, the Islamic calendar, and even the Mayan calendar by visiting the Fourmilab Calendar Converter at http://www.fourmilab.ch/documents/calendar/.

Chinese calendar systems are quite complex and have changed several times; a full discussion is far beyond the scope of this book. If you're interested, you can find information here: http://www.hermetic.ch/cal_stud/chinese_cal.htm.

On Names and Dates

Historians use "CE" (Common Era) and "BCE" (Before the Common Era) instead of the more common "AD" (Anno Domini, or Year of Our Lord) and "BC" (Before Christ), reflecting the fact that the year-numbering system established by the Gregorian calendar is used throughout the world in many countries not culturally Christian.

The CE/BCE designation dates back to at least 1708, and has been adopted as a standard by the United Nations and the Universal Postal Union. Because this series of books covers events and people of all nations and cultures, we use the CE/BCE terms.

The abbreviation "O.S." ("Old Style") on some dates refers to the fact that the Russian Empire did not switch from the Julian to the Gregorian calendar at the same time as the rest of Europe, and therefore some figures and events have two dates.

Also, in the Julian calendar in England in the 16th century, the year began on March 25 rather than January 1. To avoid confusion with Gregorian dates, dates between January and March were often written using both years.

People and events whose original names are not in the Western alphabet have their native names (where possible) in the appropriate script shown in parenthesis. If you are using an e-reader to access an electronic version of this book, all characters don't always display on all devices.

A 50-year brass perpetual calendar.

Quote of the Day

"Time is an illusion, lunchtime doubly so."

Douglas Adams,
from *The Hitchhiker's Guide to the Galaxy*

Notes
and
Credits

THE PANACEA MAGNA

Timespinner
Press

Cartoon by John T. McCutcheon

Copyright, Credit, and Contact

Follow Us

Our blog "This Day in History" (http://timespinnerpress.com/this-day-in-history/) features short articles on events and people associated with each day, and updates several times each week. Also subscribe to the "Quote of the Day" at http://timespinnerpress.com/quote-of-the-day/. You can get daily links by following us on Facebook at TimespinnerPress, or on Twitter as @sidewisethinker.

Contact Us

Find an error or a format problem? Want information about the series, about us, or about when the volume for your special day might be available? Please email us at editor@timespinnerpress.com. (We also take requests if your special day isn't yet complete. Please give us at least six weeks' notice if possible.)

Sources

We owe a great debt to Wikipedia, which is our first stop for research. We attempt to make independent confirmation of all important dates and facts through a variety of other sources.

Other sources we frequently use include the Library of Congress; "on this day" listings from *Encyclopedia Britannica*, the *New York Times*, and the BBC; Omniglot for the names of months in other languages; *Chase's Calendar of Events*; Brownielocks.com, Foodimentary, and, of course, the always essential Google.

All art and photographs are either in the public domain, used under a Creative Commons license, or with a "fair use" justification, and most frequently come from Wikimedia Commons and the Library of Congress Prints and Photographs Division.

Attribution is provided where possible, or as requested by the copyright owner, or when there is particular historical significance, listed below. For information about any particular illustration or photograph, please contact us.

Credits

1. The cover photograph, "Boulder Dam, 1941," was taken by Ansel Adams on behalf of the National Park Service, and is from the collection of the National Archives and Records Administration (ARC 519837). It is in the public domain as a work created by an employee or contractor of the US government as part of that person's official duties.
2. The illustration of the month of September used on the back cover is from the French Gothic illuminated manuscript *Les Très Riches Heures du duc de Berry* by the Limbourg Brothers, Jean Colombe, and an intermediate painter whose name is lost to history. It is in the public domain because its copyright has expired.
3. The box graphic used on the first page is from a 1916 pamphlet entitled "Divorce versus Democracy" authored by G. K. Chesterton, originally published in London by the Society of St. Peter and St. Paul. It is in the public domain in the US because it was published prior to 1923, and is in the public domain in all countries (including the country of origin) in which the copyright time is the author's life plus 70 years or less.
4. The graphic design for the section pages in this book is from a design originally created for a pharmacy label. It is courtesy of Wellcome Images (ICV No 11073, photo V0010813), and is used here under CC BY-SA 4.0.
5. The photograph "Close-Up Photograph of Boulder Dam, 1942," was taken by Ansel Adams on behalf of the National

Park Service, and is from the collection of the National Archives and Records Administration (ARC 519840). It is in the public domain as a work created by an employee or contractor of the US government as part of that person's official duties.

6. The diagram of Hoover Dam by Jarek Tuszynski of the Bureau of Reclamation is in the public domain as a as a work created by an employee or contractor of the US government as part of that person's official duties.

7. The 1932 photograph of drillers and scalers during the construction of the Hoover Dam is from the collection of the National Archives and Records Administration (ARC 293760). It is in the public domain as a work created by an employee or contractor of the US government as part of that person's official duties.

8. The postcard "Boulder Dam — Upstream Face and Intake Towers from Arizona Side" was published by Smith & Chandler, Las Vegas, as part of the "Tichnor Quality Views" line by Tichnor Bros., Inc., Boston. It is in the public domain because it was first published in the United States between 1923 and 1977 without a copyright notice.

9. The 1916 photograph of Babe Ruth is by Charles M. Conlon. It is in the public domain because its copyright has expired.

10. The US Navy photograph of USS *Nautilus* (SSN-571) is in the public domain as a work created by an employee or contractor of the US government as part of that person's official duties. US Navy Photo ID 120120-N-ZZ999-001.

11. The circa 1953 publicity photograph of James Dean is in the public domain because it was first published in the United States between 1923 and 1977 without a copyright notice. Typically, publicity photographs are not copyrighted because of the way in which they are intended to be used.

12. The 2012 photograph of Elie Wiesel is by David Shankbone. It is used here under CC BY-SA 3.0.

13. The 1959 photograph of Truman Capote was taken by Roger Higgins and is from the New York *World-Telegram and the Sun* Newspaper Photograph Collection at the Library of Congress (digital ID cph.3c19337). Per the deed of gift, the image is in the public domain.

14. The 1947 photograph of Buddy Rich by William P. Gottlieb is part of the William P. Gottlieb Collection at the Library of Congress (digital ID gottlieb.14811). In accordance with the wishes of William Gottlieb, the photographs in this collection entered the public domain in 2010.

15. The publicity photograph of Deborah Kerr and Robert Mitchum from the 1957 film *Heaven Knows, Mr. Allison*, is in the public domain because it was first published in the United States between 1923 and 1977 without a copyright notice. Typically, publicity photographs are not copyrighted because of the way in which they are intended to be used.

16. The 1997 photograph of Martina Hingis was taken by PH1(AW) M. Clayton Farrington. It is in the public domain as a work created by an officer or employee of the US militaryas part of that person's official duties. This photograph won the Military Photographer of the Year Award in 1997. It is courtesy defenseimagery.mil, ID DN-SP-98-03532.

17. The photograph of Les Paul and Mary Ford originally appeared on the cover of *TV Guide* Magazine, January 22-29, 1954. It is in the public domain because it was published in the United States between 1923 and 1963, and although there was an original copyright, the copyright was not renewed.

18. The 1941 publicity photograph of Edgar Bergen with Mortimer Snerd is in the public domain because it was first published in the United States between 1923 and 1977 without a copyright notice. Typically, publicity photographs are not copyrighted because of the way in which they are intended to be used.

19. The painting "St. Jerome" by El Greco was painted prior to 1614 and is in the public domain because its copyright has expired. The painting is in the collection of the Scottish National Gallery.

20. The 19th century portrait of José María Morelos by Vicente Guijosa Aguirre is in the public domain because its copyright has expired.

21. The 1878 painting "Jews Praying in the Synagogue on Yom Kippur" is in the public domain because its copyright has expired. It is courtesy Tel Aviv Museum of Art.

22. The painting "September" is from the *Brevarium Grimani,* circa 1510, and is in the public domain because its copyright has expired.

23. The photograph of a star sapphire was released into the public domain by its author, Mitchell Gore.

24. The chromolithograph of a forget-me-not is by Louis-Aristide Léon Constans and originally appeared in the 1852-1853 edition of *Paxton's Flower Garden.* It is in the public domain because its copyright has expired.

25. The celestial sphere is from *Scenography of the Ptolemaic Cosmography,* by Johannes van Loon, based on Andreas Cellarius's *Harmonia Macrocosmica,* 1660. It is in the public domain because its copyright has expired.

26. The 1906 automobile calendar is by Edward Penfield, and is in the collection of the Library of Congress Prints and Photographs Division. It is in the public domain because its copyright has expired.

27. The 50-year perpetual calendar photograph is in the public domain.

28. The cartoon by John T. McCutcheon is from his 1905 collection *The Mysterious Stranger and Other Cartoons* by John T. McCutcheon. It is in the public domain because its copyright has expired.

License Description and Terms

Aside from material purely in the public domain, photographs and other material in this book are used under specific licenses permitting free use, usually with an attribution requirement. For full text and terms of these licenses, click or enter the appropriate links below. If you believe there is an error in the copyright status or attribution of any of these images, please email us.

- Creative Commons Attribution 2.0 Generic (CC-BY 2.0): http://creativecommons.org/licenses/by/2.0/deed.en

Timespinner
Press

Other Books from Timespinner Press

The Story of a Special Day
Michael Dobson

A series of (eventually) 366 volumes covering everything that happened on your special day! Events, births, deaths, quotes, holidays, and much more. It's like a birthday card they'll never throw away!

US$7.95 print / US$2.99 ebook.

From Plassey to Pakistan
Humayun Mirza

The history of British Colonial India and the formation of Pakistan from the unique perspective of the son of Pakistan's first president and last of the royal line of Bengal, Bihar, and Orissa! This unique historical document tells the inside story of this distinguished family, including the detailed story of the coup that toppled his father from power!

US$27.95 print

A Whole New Navy: America's War in the Pacific

Miles Durr

The most comprehensive and detailed description of America's naval war in the Pacific ever—every battle, every ship, every task force and every task group from Pearl Harbor through the Japanese surrender! A must-have for the collection of every World War II buff!

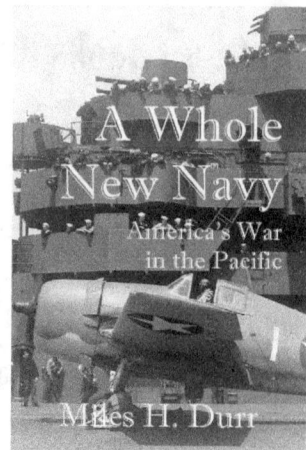

US$29.95 print

Improbable History: The Weird, the Obscure, and the Strangely Important

edited by Michael Dobson

From the birth of Western civilization to the rescue of Apollo 13, from the Leaning Tower of Pisa to Florence's Duomo, history has often turned on small, improbable details. Whatever happened to the ancient Samaritan people? Why did a fortuitous rainstorm allow the British to conquer India? How did an air raid in Italy lead to the development of chemotherapy? What happened when Albert Einstein met Adolf Hitler on the streets of Berlin? How did the Japanese manage to attack the US mainland using balloons? A cast of award-winning writers tackle some of the strangest tales in history!

US$19.95 print